Well Read 2

SKILLS AND STRATEGIES FOR READING

Instructor's Pack

Kate Dobiecka | Karen Wiederholt

SERIES CONSULTANTS

Mindy Pasternak | Elisaveta Wrangell

OXFORD
UNIVERSITY PRESS

OXFORD
UNIVERSITY PRESS

198 Madison Avenue
New York, NY 10016 USA

Great Clarendon Street, Oxford OX2 6DP UK

Oxford University Press is a department of the University of Oxford.
It furthers the University's objective of excellence in research, scholarship,
and education by publishing worldwide in

Oxford New York

Auckland Cape Town Dar es Salaam Hong Kong Karachi
Kuala Lumpur Madrid Melbourne Mexico City Nairobi
New Delhi Shanghai Taipei Toronto

With offices in

Argentina Austria Brazil Chile Czech Republic France Greece
Guatemala Hungary Italy Japan Poland Portugal Singapore
South Korea Switzerland Thailand Turkey Ukraine Vietnam

OXFORD and OXFORD ENGLISH are registered trademarks of
Oxford University Press

Editorial Director: Sally Yagan
Senior Publishing Manager: Pietro Alongi
Senior Managing Editor: Patricia O'Neill
Head of Development and Project Editors: Karen Horton
Associate Development Editor: Beverley Langevine
Design Director: Robert Carangelo
Design Project Manager: Maj-Britt Hagsted
Project Manager: Allison Harm
Production Manager: Shanta Persaud
Production Controller: Zai Jawat Ali

ISBN: 978 0 19 476111 6 (instructor's pack)
ISBN: 978 0 19 476114 7 (answer key)
Printed in Hong Kong.
10 9 8 7 6 5 4 3 2 1

Contents

Notes to the Teacher iv

PowerPoint® Teaching Tool iv

ExamView® Test Generator vii

Answer Key 1

    Chapter 1 1

    Chapter 2 3

    Chapter 3 5

    Chapter 4 7

    Chapter 5 10

    Chapter 6 12

    Chapter 7 14

    Chapter 8 17

Notes to the Teacher

Welcome to **Well Read**, a four-level series that teaches and reinforces crucial reading skills and vocabulary strategies step-by-step through a wide range of authentic texts that are meant to engage students' (and teachers') interest. **Well Read 2 Instructor's Pack** is intended for instructors using **Well Read 2** in their low-intermediate level classrooms. All of the texts in **Well Read 2** are at the 7.0–8.0 Flesch-Kincaid Grade Level, and the student book contains 24–48 hours of instructional material, depending on how much in-class work is assigned.

In the **Well Read Instructor's Pack**, you will find two technological resources that will enhance your students' classroom experience: the **PowerPoint® Teaching Tool** and the **ExamView® Test Generator**. In addition, you will find the answer key to the student book.

PowerPoint® Teaching Tool

This data CD includes a set of fully integrated PowerPoint® slides that serve as a valuable class management tool. These visual aids contain every activity of the student book except for the texts themselves, which students read in their books. The corresponding student book page numbers are always included in the bottom right portion of each slide.

The slides also contain all answers to text questions, and can be used as an answer key in class. The **Instructor's Pack** also indicates where each activity can be found on the PowerPoint® slides with an icon ( ) that includes the slide number.

Given that the visual aids replicate, magnify, and provide color to the images in the text, they are intended to be used along with the student book to accommodate a **"heads up/heads down"** methodological approach with students looking both down at their books and up at the visual aids as directed by the instructor. For example, the texts are strictly a "heads down" activity, while reviewing the answers is "heads up."

Questions can have one of three types of answers: (1) no answer, usually because there are many possibilities, or it is a discussion question; (2) an answer or several possible answers; or (3) a click and type answer box in which the instructor can type an answer, several possible answers, a survey, etc.

CHAPTER INTRODUCTION WITH POWERPOINT®

In each chapter of the student book, the opening page introduces the chapter's theme. The questions and photographs are designed to activate the students' prior knowledge, as well as stimulate some limited discussion before the previewing, reading, and post-reading activities.

( ) The PowerPoint® slides contain the introduction page of the text over several slides. Students view this material with their books open or closed. Answers are provided at the click of the mouse.

GETTING STARTED WITH POWERPOINT®

This activity precedes each text or graphic component in the student book. It is designed to help students focus in on a more specific topic through reflection and discussion. It also introduces a small number of critical vocabulary words or phrases.

The PowerPoint® slides can be used to present this activity or students can use their books initially and then the slides can be used for a classroom discussion of partner results. Answers are provided at the click of the mouse. Some questions have a box following them instead of an answer. On every slide that contains a box, **"click and type option"** is noted. Here, the instructor can enter answers elicited from students on the slides without pulling up the screen to write on the blackboard. To type in the box, click anywhere inside the box. The answers that are entered will remain until the PowerPoint® file is closed. They will remain permanently if the file is saved before closing, making it easy to see which activities have been covered in a given class. It is recommended that you save a copy and rename the file in order to retain a clean version of each chapter.

These **click and type** boxes are not only useful in order to type student responses, but they can also be used to try out and then erase possibilities. The *backspace* key works in the same way as with a word processor. Finally, the number of students who answered a question a certain way can be recorded in the boxes in survey format.

ACTIVE PREVIEWING WITH POWERPOINT®

Active Previewing asks students to read only brief and selected parts of the text, and then answer very simple questions that focus on this material. This activity encourages the notion that students do not have to understand each and every word of what they are reading. There is a strong emphasis on how to preview a wide range of genres, both academic and non-academic, including—but not limited to—newspaper articles, online texts, magazine articles, textbook articles, tables, charts, graphs, timelines, and graphics.

The PowerPoint® slides can be used to get this activity started and to review

the answers. For each set of questions, all the questions are shown first and then the answers come up one at a time. In this way, the entire activity can be done "heads up."

READING AND RECALLING WITH POWERPOINT®

The first reading activity asks students to read and recall. This is less daunting than being presented with an entire text, and also allows the students to retain more. Recalling encourages students to be accountable for the material they read. At its most basic, students build their short-term memories. On a deeper level, students begin to process information more quickly and holistically. Perfect recall is never the goal.

The PowerPoint® slides contain the directions for this activity. The textbook is needed for the actual readings.

UNDERSTANDING THE TEXT WITH POWERPOINT®

After each text, students are presented with a two-part reading comprehension activity. The first part checks the students' comprehension of the most basic ideas expressed in the text, whereas the second part challenges the students to recall other key ideas and information.

With the PowerPoint® slides for this activity, the text doesn't need to be opened at all.

READING SKILLS WITH POWERPOINT®

Among other essential reading skills, students are introduced to topic, main idea, and supporting details in separate chapters, which allows them to practice and master each of these skills before progressing to the next. Earlier chapters present choices in a multiple choice fashion, whereas subsequent chapters require the students to write their own interpretations. The ability to think critically about the information that is presented in the text is a crucial part of being an active reader. Students are first taught to distinguish between facts and opinions, and later, inferences. In the final chapters of the student book, students will be asked to find facts and opinions and to make inferences of their own.

The PowerPoint® slides contain all the material from the **Reading Skills** boxes, so the instructor can take advantage of these slides to teach each reading skill.

VOCABULARY STRATEGIES WITH POWERPOINT®

Students first learn that they can understand the general idea of the text even without understanding every word; however, skipping words is not always an option, thus students are introduced to different strategies that can help them determine the meanings of new vocabulary without using their dictionaries. The various vocabulary strategies are presented and then reinforced in later chapters. All vocabulary activities present the vocabulary as it is used in the texts themselves, yet the vocabulary strategies that are taught can be applied universally to reading that the students do outside class. Developing these strategies will allow students to become more autonomous readers.

The PowerPoint® slides contain all the material from the **Vocabulary Strategies** boxes and can be used to guide the class through the activities in this section. Both questions and answers are provided so this can be a "heads up" activity.

DISCUSSING THE ISSUES WITH POWERPOINT®

Every text ends with a series of questions that encourage the students to express their opinions and ideas about the general subject discussed in the text. The questions are designed to be communicative in that they strike upon compelling issues raised in the text.

The PowerPoint® slides provide the questions from this discussion activity. The instructor can use these slides to remind students to keep on target.

PUTTING IT ON PAPER WITH POWERPOINT®

Reading and writing are two skills that inherently go together. The writing activity complements the chapter texts, yet it is also designed to stand independently should the instructor decide not to read all of the chapter texts. Each *Putting It On Paper* activity offers two writing prompts; the instructor can allow students to choose between the prompts or can select one prompt for all students to use.

The PowerPoint® slides contain all the material from this section to facilitate discussion and review. Therefore this activity can be "heads up" to give students the directions and "heads down" to do the writing.

TAKING IT ONLINE WITH POWERPOINT®

Each *Taking It Online* activity guides the students through the steps necessary for conducting online research, based on the theme of the chapter. Instructors might opt to prescreen a select number of websites in advance, thus directing the students to more reliable and useful sites. *Taking It Online* finishes with a follow-up activity that enables the students to take their research one step further, in pairs or groups.

The PowerPoint® slides contain the text material to support this section. A particularly valuable feature of the click and type option for this section is their use for entering Website addresses. Instructors can pre-select particularly worthwhile Websites to enter into these locations and the students can copy them. Alternatively, the file can be saved and that slide can be printed out and copied for dissemination. Given the complexity of some Web addresses, that can be a way to avoid errors and frustration.

ADDITIONAL TIPS FOR USING THE POWERPOINT® SLIDES

The use of the slides can foster an enjoyable, effective and efficient classroom experience. That they follow the textbook exactly means that the coordination between text activities and the visual aids is seamless. Instructors find that the use of this teaching tool facilitates many aspects of teaching, especially planning. This total class management tool takes the instructor and class step-by-step through each chapter.

In the best case scenario, a instructor would turn on the projector and keep it on throughout class and let the slides guide the way through each activity in the chapters. For the classroom in which the use of a projector is limited, one could use the slides to begin the chapter, for the **Understanding the Text** section and also to go over all answers. In either case, the ability to have students in the ""heads up"" mode can add a great deal to the dynamic in the classroom. The instructor can see the faces of the students and read their expressions for understanding or a lack of it. Students enjoy the beautiful art and photos and often pay more attention than they would with only a textbook.

If a computer/projection system is not available, overhead transparencies could be made to simulate the experience.

ExamView® Test Generator

This CD-ROM enables you to create customized reading skills tests for use with **Well Read 2**. You can use these tests to assess student progress at any phase of the learning process: pre-test, chapter-by-chapter, or final exam. This tool will help you evaluate the effectiveness of your teaching, and it will allow your students to gauge their own progress based on their test results.

A large selection of questions in familiar question formats are featured on the CD-ROM: multiple choice, true/false, completion, and essay. The questions are always based on the skills and strategies covered in the corresponding student book chapter. In the **Banks** folder, there is a folder called *Well Read 2 OUP*, in which you will find **Question Banks** for each chapter of *Well Read 2*.

There are many ways to create tests using this CD-ROM:

Create a test in just minutes: Use the *QuickTest Wizard* to select the type and number of questions you want to include from the question banks in the Banks folder.

Select specific questions: Use the *Test Builder* to navigate your way through the question banks in the Banks folder, and pick specific questions to include on your test.

Write your own questions: Create completely new tests using your own questions or edit the questions provided. In order for these questions to be available at a later time, they need to be added to the Bank file.

Important note: In *ExamView Assessment Suite®*, the reading passage is designed to appear with each different question type. For example, if you choose multiple choice, completion, and essay questions, the reading passage will appear three times. If you want the reading passage to appear only once at the beginning of each test, simply highlight and delete the other reading passages once you have finished creating your test.

All tests can be printed out for students to take at their desks. Test questions can be scrambled to appear in any order, multiple versions of a test can be created, and you can save all your tests on your computer to use for future classes. An answer key is automatically generated for each test you create.

Alternatively, tests may be administered by computer or online through a school website for an additional fee. The *ExamView®* website (www.examview.com) provides instructions for computer and online testing. You can also subscribe to the *ExamView®* Testing Center for access to a variety of services.

For easy, step-by-step instructions for using **Well Read 2 ExamView® Test Generator**, see the **Manual** on the CD-ROM.

Answer Key

4 **SB p. 1 Introduction**
2.
a. ship
b. train
c. wagon train

Text 1 Keep Running

8 **SB p. 3 Skipping Words**
1. b
2. a
3. b
4. a

10 **SB p. 3 Active Previewing**

A.

Rosie Swale Pope / a woman who has run from Wales, across Europe and Russia and now is in the U.S. / a woman whose goal is to run across the world

12 **SB p. 4 Understanding the Text**

A.
1. b
2. a
3. c
4. a
5. a

Text 2 Houses on Wheels

18 **SB p. 6 Skipping Words**

A.
1. recreational vehicle: noun
2. compatible: adjective
3. regretted: verb; extreme: adjective; shift: noun; lifestyle: noun
4. swivels: verb; windshield: noun
5. diesel fuel: noun; costly: adjective; fuel-efficient: adjective

19 **SB p. 7 Active Previewing**
1. people who travel around and live in their vehicle
2. An RV is a recreational vehicle. A nomad is a person who wanders and does not have a permanent home.

21 **SB p. 8 Understanding the Text**

A.
1. c
2. a
3. b

B.
1. F
2. F
3. T
4. T
5. F

23 **SB p. 9 Discussing the Issues**
1. The Webers say that the traveling, the scenery, and the food are the advantages. The disadvantages are the small space and the cost of diesel fuel.

Text 3 Moving Westward

27 **SB p. 9 Active Previewing**
1. The Pioneer Trails; The title means: the trails that emigrants (pioneers) took as they explored west.
2. North America / United States
3. historic trails

30 **SB p. 11 Scanning**
1. California Trail, Gila Trail, Mormon Trail, Oregon Trail, and Oregon / Santa Fe Trail
2. the Morman trail
3. the Morman trail
4. New Mexico
5. Santa Fe Trail to Gila Trail; Oregon / California Trail to California Trail

Text 4 Laying the Rails

35 SB p. 12 Skipping Words

A.
1. migration: noun
2. Civil War: noun; veterans: noun; Union Pacific: noun
3. endured: verb
4. avalanches: noun; explosions: noun
5. route: noun; wealthy: adjective; Mormon: noun; communities: noun

36 SB p. 12 Active Previewing
1. Western Migration; the building of the railroads in America to travel from the east coast to California
2. history; sociology

38 SB p. 14 Understanding the Text

A.
1. a
2. c
3. b
4. c
5. b

B.
1. Central Pacific
2. Central Pacific
3. Union Pacific
4. Central Pacific
5. Union pacific (although both probably endured the heat)

3 SB p. 17 Introduction

2.
a. Indian tiger
b. northern white rhino
c. sea turtle
d. giant panda

Text 1 A Famous Endangered Animal

7 SB p. 19 Skipping Words

1. noun
2. noun
3. verb
4. verb
5. verb

9 SB p. 19 Active Previewing

1. giant pandas
2. China
3. It is trying to breed Pandas to increase the population.
4. giant pandas; the giant panda is an endangered species; how organizations are trying to save the giant panda

11 SB p. 21 Understanding the Text

A.
b
B.
1. a
2. c
3. c
4. a
5. b

15 SB p. 22 Understanding Vocabulary in Context—Definitions

A.
1. a; a plant or animal with such a low population that it might become extinct
2. a; a place where a plant or animal normally lives
3. a; what it eats
4. b; return back to

Text 2 Studying Tigers

21 SB p. 24 Skipping Words

1. naturalists; noun
2. preservation; noun
3. destruction; noun
4. designated; verb
5. factors; noun

22 SB p. 24 Active Previewing

1. endangered tigers in India; protecting tigers in India
2. yes

24 SB p. 26 Understanding the Text

1. c
2. b
3. c
4. a

25 SB p. 26 Understanding Vocabulary in Context—Definitions

A.
the illegal hunting of animals

B.
1. conference: professional meeting, often at a big hotel
2. eliminated: stopped, removed
3. encourage: help someone want to do something
4. estimate: guess
5. feline: cat
6. reduced: made smaller

Text 3 Animals in Danger

30 SB p. 27 Active Previewing

1. Endangered Species of the World
2. mammals, birds, reptiles, amphibians, fish, insects, other invertebrates
3. 100 different species

33 SB p. 26 Scanning

1. amphibians
2. reptiles
3. over 1200
4. 1100
5. about 7800

Text 4   Discovered Again

36 SB p. 29 Getting Started

a. mammoth
b. ivory-billed woodpecker
c. coelacanth
d. dodo
e. servaline genet

The mammoth and the dodo are extinct.

37 SB p. 30 Skipping Words

1. ecosystem; noun
2. colony; noun
3. ancient; adjective

38 SB p. 30 Active Previewing

1. animals thought to be extinct that have been seen again
2. ivory-billed woodpecker/servaline genet/ cahow/coelacanth
3. in a science class

40 SB p. 31 Understanding the Text

A.

1. c
2. c
3. c
4. a
5. c

B.

1. Arkansas; 60 years; 2005
2. Tanzania; 70 years/since 1932; 2002
3. Bermuda; more than 300 years/since the 1600s; 1951
4. South Africa; 65 million years; 1938

43 SB p. 30 Understanding Vocabulary in Context—Definitions

A.

a camera left in the wilderness to photograph an animal

B.

1. found again
2. animals that only eat meat
3. a collection of bones preserved in rock

3 SB p. 35 Introduction

2.
a. pumpkin seeds: pumpkins
b. flower bulbs: flowers
c. peanuts

Text 1 Giant Pumpkins

5 SB p. 36 Getting Started

B.

1, 3, 6, 8

6 SB p. 36 Skipping Words

1. champion: noun; consecutive: adjective;
    mere: adjective
2. genetics: noun; trial: noun; error: noun
3. inherited: verb
4. essential: adjective

7 SB p. 37 Active Previewing

1. Howard Dill
2. giant pumpkins
3. Nova Scotia, Canada
4. 1979 to 1982

8 SB p. 37 Scanning

1. 90
2. 442
3. Larry Checkon
4. 493.5 pounds
5. ten

10 SB p. 39 Understanding the Text

A.

1. a
2. b
3. b
4. c
5. a

B.

4 a
5 b
1 c
3 d
6 e
2 f

Text 2 The Garden on Robben Island

15 SB p. 40 Getting Started

1. Nelson Mandela was the president of South
    Africa from 1994-1999.
2. He was in prison because of his actions in the
    1960s against the apartheid government.
3. He was in prison for 27 years: 18 years at
    Robben Island.
4. Mandela enjoyed writing, reading books,
    listening to music, and gardening.

16 SB p. 40 Skipping Words

1. excavate: verb
2. tend: verb; enduring: adjective
3. custodian: noun
4. metaphor: noun

17 SB p. 41 Active Previewing

1. Nelson Mandela's
2. Mandela's garden while he was in prison

19 SB p. 42 Understanding the Text

A.

1. T
2. F
3. T
4. F
5. T

B.

1. b
2. a
3. c
4. c
5. b

22 SB p. 44 Understanding Subject and
Object Pronouns

1. the authorities
2. comrades
3. peanuts
4. Mandela's attempt to grow peanuts
5. a leader
6. seeds

Text 3 Bulb Planting

[25] SB p. 44 Getting Started
3.
a, c, d, e, j

[27] SB p. 45 Active Previewing
1. Spring Flowering Bulbs
2. when and how much a flowering bulb grows
3. measuring and comparing flowering bulb growth

[29] SB p. 47 Scanning
1. 6"; 1'–5'; April
2. tulip; 7"
3. giant allium; 4'
4. crocus; early March
5. giant allium; late May

[30] SB p. 47 Discussing the Issues
1. Taller plants bloom later. Gardeners should plant the bulbs of taller plants 3" to 4" deeper.

Text 4 Orchid Obsession

[33] SB p. 48 Getting Started
1. F
2. F
3. F
4. T
5. T
6. F

[34] SB p. 48 Active Previewing
1. the history of orchid hunting (collecting)
2. a very strong interest in orchids; an obsession with orchids

[35] SB p. 49 Scanning
1. 1908
2. 1800s; when orchids were not mass-produced
3. Tom Hart-Dyke

[37] SB p. 51 Understanding the Text
A.
1. a
2. c
3. c
4. b
5. a
6. c

B.
1. England; 1830s; botanist, made a container to transport plants overseas
2. Czechoslovakia (Czech Republic); discovered 800 new orchid species
3. England; 1800s; painted thousands of orchid pictures
4. England; 2000s; was kidnapped while hunting for orchids / attempted to find a new orchid species to name after his grandmother

[40] SB p. 52 Understanding Subject Pronouns
1. orchids
2. European orchid hunters
3. Benedict Roezl
4. the one orchid hunter left alive after the tragic 1908 expedition
5. orchid hunting
6. Tom Hart-Dyke

[42] SB p. 53 Understanding Vocabulary in Context—Synonyms and Definitions
1. a; exotic and fascinating flower
2. c; fascinating
3. a; a strangley strong interest in orchids
4. c; rich
5. c; faraway
6. a; the people of that area
7. b; grown in large amounts in big, controlled areas
8. c; available

[44] SB p. 54 Discussing the Issues
1. Orchids grew in remote areas, were difficult to transport and difficult to grow. They are less expensive now because they are mass-produced.

3 **SB p. 57 Introduction**

2.
a. swimming
b. running
c. bicycling

Text 1 A Three-in-One Sport

5 **SB p. 58 Getting Started**

A.
2. athletic competition; swimming, bicycling, and running

7 **SB p. 58 Active Previewing**

1. training for the Ironman competition
2. every October in Hawaii

8 **SB p. 58 Scanning**

1. 2.4 miles
2. 7 a.m.
3. 18-24 hours each week

10 **SB p. 60 Understanding the Text**

A.
1. b
2. c
3. a
4. b
5. a

B.
1. F
2. T
3. F
4. F
5. T

14 **SB p. 61 Understanding the Topic**

A.
1.
a. G
b. T
c. S

B.
1.
a. T

b. G
c. S
2.
a. S
b. T
c. G
3.
a. G
b. S
c. T

16 **SB p. 62 Understanding Vocabulary in Context—Definitions**

1. 26.2 mile race
2. ability to perform for a long period of time
3. healthy eating
4. goal
5. crazy

Text 2 Athletes in Training

21 **SB p. 63 Active Previewing**

1. strange training methods of athletes
2. Chuchei Nambu, Tegla Loroupe, Katerina Neumannova, and Lynne Cox

22 **SB p. 63 Scanning**

1. Lynne Cox
2. Chuchei Nambu; Japanese
3. Katerina Neummanova; cross-country skiing
4. Kenyan; marathon running

24 **SB p. 65 Understanding the Text**

A.
1. Lynne Cox
2. Tegla Laroupe
3. Chuchei Nambu
4. Katerina Neumannova

B.
1. Lynne Cox; Katerina Neumannova
2. Tegla Loroupe; Chuchei Nambu
3. Tegla Loroupe; Chuchei Nambu; Katerina Neumannova
4. Chuchei Nambu; Katerina Neumannova
5. Lynne Cox; Katerina Neumannova

26 SB p. 66 Understanding the Topic

A.

1.
   a. T
   b. G
   c. S

B.

1.
   a. G
   b. S
   c. T
2.
   a. G
   b. T
   c. S
3.
   a. S
   b. T
   c. G

28 SB p. 67 Understanding Vocabulary in Context—Definitions

1. a part of a relay race
2. a race run by four athletes, one after the other
3. closely watched
4. control (cattle's) movement as a group
5. low-oxygen

Text 3 Marathon Times

35 SB p. 69 Active Previewing

1. Record Marathon Times
2. men's record times/women's record times
3. 1900

36 SB p. 70 Scanning

A.

1. 2:08
2. 2:15
3. 1972
4. 36 seconds
5. 10 seconds

B.

1. b
2. c
3. b
4. b

38 SB p. 71 Understanding Vocabulary in Context—Synonyms

1. a
2. c
3. b
4. b
5. a
6. c

Text 4 Special Olympics

43 SB p. 73 Active Previewing

1. athletes with intellectual disabilities
2. 150 different countries
3. Researchers found that there are many benefits to being in the Special Olympics program.
4. 2004 and 2005

44 SB p. 73 Scanning

1. 26
2. University of Massachusetts and University of Utah
3. 52%

46 SB p. 75 Understanding the Text

A.
1. F
2. T
3. F
4. F
5. T

B.
1, 2, 6, 7, 8, 9

48 SB p. 75 Understanding the Topic

A.
1.
a. G
b. T
c. S

B.
1.
a. T
b. G
c. S
2.
a. S
b. G
c. T
3.
a. T
b. S
c. G

50 SB p. 76 Understanding Subject Pronouns

1. researchers
2. Special Olympics athletes
3. the research study
4. Special Olympics athletes
5. athletes that have left the Special Olympics program

3 SB p. 79 Introduction

2.
a. moveable type
b. computer
c. runner

Text 1 Baby Sign Language

5 SB p. 80 Getting Started

A.
1. babbling, crying, yawning
3. using sign language

7 SB p. 80 Active Previewing

1. communication for babies who cannot talk; baby sign language
2. baby sign language allows Emma to communicate her needs with her parents; Emma uses baby sign language to tell her parents exactly what she wants

9 SB p. 82 Understanding the Text

1. b
2. c
3. c
4. b
5. a
6. c

11 SB p. 83 Understanding Subject and Object Pronouns

1. I: subject pronoun
2. it: object pronoun
3. she: subject pronoun; us: object pronoun
4. we: subject pronoun
5. we: subject pronoun; she: subject pronoun
6. us: object pronoun
7. me: object pronoun; them: object pronoun

12 SB p. 83 Understanding the Topic

1.
a. G
b. S
c. T

14 SB p. 84 Understanding the Main Idea

A.
1.
a. G
b. MI
c. S

B.
1.
a. G
b. MI
c. S
2.
a. S
b. G
c. MI
3.
a. MI
b. G
c. S
4.
a. G
b. MI
c. S

Text 2 The Whistle Language

21 SB p. 86 Active Previewing

1. the whistle language of La Gomera; Silbo Gomera
2. La Gomera
3. school children in La Gomera

23 SB p. 88 Understanding the Text

1. b
2. a
3. a
4. b
5. c
6. a

25 SB p. 89 Understanding the Topic and Main Idea

1. a
2. c

27 SB p. 89 Understanding Vocabulary in Context—Apposition

A.
1. a small island off the coast of Africa
2. the shepherds

Text 3   Advances in Communication

32 SB p. 91 Active Previewing
1. the history of communication
2. B.C.E. and C.E.
3. 5500 years (3500 + 2000)

33 SB p. 92 Understanding the Timeline
1. a
2. a
3. b
4. b
5. a

Text 4   Communication Technology

38 SB p. 93 Active Previewing
1. Internet use; facts and trends of Internet communication
2. teens and adults
3. United States
4. It's happening now.

39 SB p. 93 Scanning
1. e-mail
2. e-mail on Fridays
3. Instant Messaging

41 SB p. 95 Understanding the Text
A.
1. T
2. F
3. T
4. T
5. F

B.
FACTS
2. 91% of adults use email.
3. Employees at U.S. companies have to deal with three times the amount of e-mail they did in 1999.
4. 87% of teens use the Internet.
5. In the last four years, teen use of the Internet has increased by 24%.
TRENDS
2. Employers institute email-free days.
3. Employers build common areas, meeting spaces, and conference rooms, and spend more money on business travel.
4. More and more parents send their children to low-tech camps or to study abroad.
5. Teens and adults use new technologies such as Instant Messaging and text messaging in order to connect with friends.

43 SB p. 96 Understanding the Main Idea
1. Internet use is up in all age groups.
2. Employers and parents are responding by finding ways to give people breaks from technology in order to encourage face-to-face interactions.
3. Because Internet use in the United States is up in all age groups, employers and parents are responding by finding ways to give people breaks from technology in order to encourage face-to-face interactions.

3 SB p. 99 Introduction

2.
a. natural medicine
b. vitamin and mineral supplements
c. herbal remedies

Text 1   International Cure

6 SB p. 100 Active Previewing

Qian Ceng Ta; effective herbal treatment for Alzheimer's

8 SB p. 102 Understanding the Text

A.
1. b
2. a
3. c
4. a
5. b

B.
1. treats Alzheimer's disease; improves brain functioning; damages the stomach and liver
2. treats Alzheimer's disease; improves brain functioning; does not have negative effects on the body

12 SB p. 102 Understanding Supporting Details

1. b, c
2. a, b, c
3. b
4. a, b, c

Text 2   Do Herbs Really Work?

17 SB p. 104 Active Previewing

1. echinacea; echinacea's effectiveness
2. Echinacea is not clinically effective in lessening cold symptoms.

19 SB p. 106 Understanding the Text

1. b
2. a
3. b

21 SB p. 107 Understanding Possessive Adjectives

1. possessive adjective: his, noun: Ronald Turner
2. possessive adjective: their, noun: volunteers

22 SB p. 107 Understanding Supporting Details

A.
2, 3, 5, 6

Text 3   Food Cures

26 SB p. 107 Active Previewing

1. problems, foods to try, why/how they work, how much to eat, what to avoid
2. 6

29 SB p. 108 Scanning

1. processed meats, MSG, red wine, chocolate, hard cheeses
2. one and a half cups of cooked quinoa daily
3. tea (black, green or oolong)

Text 4   Caffeine

32 SB p. 110 Getting Started

A.
1. c
2. a
3. d
4. b

B.
d

34 SB p. 111 Active Previewing

1. F
2. T
3. T
4. T

36 SB p. 114 Understanding the Text

A.
1. b, c
2. b, c
3. a, b, c
4. a
5. a, b, c
6. b

B.
1. 20 mg per ounce
2. Milk chocolate
3. 115 mg
4. between 38 mg and 71.2 mg
5. 12 oz. iced tea

39 SB p. 115 Understanding Apposition

1. one cup
2. the brain and spinal cord
3. a single can of soda or cup of coffee
4. several cups of coffee

40 SB p. 115 Understanding Vocabulary in Context—Definitions

A.
1. b; added, not natural
2. c; bad tasting
3. c; enough for one, not too much

B.
1. an illness that causes difficulty in breathing
2. a unit of measuring weight equal to 2240 pounds
3. every year
4. makes a part of the body active
5. the painful or unpleasant effects of giving up a drug you are dependent on

42 SB p. 116 Understanding Supporting Details

1. a drug produced in leaves and seeds of many plants/a drug produced artificially/part of the same group of drugs sometimes used to treat asthma/a drug that stimulates the nervous system (makes the heart beat faster, makes people feel awake and energetic, makes some people feel happy)/it tastes bitter
2. amount of caffeine in foods and drinks varies/higher doses of caffeine can cause anxiety, dizziness, headaches, and the jitters/caffeine can make it hard to sleep/caffeine is addictive and may cause withdrawal symptoms/you may feel its effect for up to six hours
3. effects vary from person to person/doctors recommend consuming no more than 100 mg of caffeine daily

3 SB p. 119 Introduction

2.
a. zoology
b. botany
c. biology

Text 1 The Work of One Scientist

6 SB p. 120 Active Previewing

1. forest canopy walkways; accessing forest canopies
2. the title and the last sentence of the last paragraph are related because they both are about ways to access the tops of the trees (heavens)

8 SB p. 122 Understanding the Text

A.
1. b
2. c
3. a

B.
2. single-rope technique and/or building walkways
3. building walkways
4. getting a grant, building inexpensive walkways
5. network of walkways grows every year

10 SB p. 123 Understanding Possessive Adjectives

¶1 possessive adjectives: their/their/their; noun/noun phrase it refers to: trees/trees/monkeys and birds
¶2 possessive adjectives: my/my/my; noun/noun phrase it refers to: Margaret Lowman/Margaret Lowman/Margaret Lowman
¶3 possessive adjectives: our/our; noun/noun phrase it refers to: Margaret Lowman and Bart Bouricius
¶4 possessive adjectives: our; noun/noun phrase it refers to: Margaret Lowman and the people she works with

12 SB p. 124 Detecting Sequence with Sequence Markers

Then, like a gift from heaven, a letter came to me one day from an arborist in nearby Amherst.
Later, we received a small grant from a local foundation interested in environmental concerns.
Finally, with a price tag less than that of most microscopes, the walkway proved an excellent investment for the advancement of science.

14 SB p. 124 Understanding Vocabulary in Context—Examples

Comparative studies are now possible in places like Australia, Samoa, North America, Central America, and South America. Even Africa boasts a walkway site in Uganda.

Text 2 Accidental Discovery

19 SB p. 125 Scanning

"One sometimes finds what one is not looking for," remarked Fleming in typically understated fashion.
"Nature makes penicillin, I just found it," he said at the time.
The quotations show his approach to science and his humility.

20 SB p. 125 Active Previewing

penicillin; Alexander Fleming's discovery of penicillin

22 SB p. 127 Understanding the Text

A.
1. b
2. c
3. b

B.
1. yes
2. not found in the text
3. yes
4. not found in the text

24 SB p. 127 Detecting Sequence with Sequence Markers

A.
1. WWI
2. early 1920s
3. 1928
4. WWII

B.
early 1920s: lysozyme
1928: penicillin

C.
1. First, Fleming had sneezed into a bacteria-laced petri-dish.
2. Several days later, he noticed that the bacteria had been destroyed by the mucus.
3. Several years later, he discovered penicillin.

26 SB p. 128 Understanding Vocabulary in Context—Examples
1. Tears; an example of bodily fluid.
2. amoxicillin and tetracycline; examples of antibiotics

Text 3   How Much Sleep Do We Need?

30 SB p. 129 Active Previewing
1. Counting Sleep; the title refers to counting how many hours of sleep an animal needs
2. the size of the animal gets larger as you look from left to right
3. the hours of sleep decrease as you look from left to right

32 SB p. 131 Scanning
1. opossum; 18 hours
2. elephant; 3 hours
3. 8 hours

Text 4   Stomach Trouble Cured

35 SB p. 131 Getting Started
1. c
2. a
3. d
4. b

37 SB p. 132 Skimming
1. Warren: 68; Marshall: 54
2. 2005
3. $1.3 million
4. 90 percent
5. 1979

38 SB p. 132 Active Previewing
1. Dr. J. Robin Warren's and Dr. Barry J. Marshall's important discovery that stomach ulcers are caused by bacteria; why Dr. J. Robin Warren and Dr. Barry J. Marshall won the 2005 Nobel Prize in Medicine
2. Two Australian researchers discovered that a bacterium, not stress or spicy food, causes stomach ulcers.

40 SB p. 134 Understanding the Text
A.
1. b
2. b
3. c

B.
1. T
2. F
3. F
4. T
5. F
6. T

42 SB p. 135 Understanding Supporting Details

1.
a. They found a bacterium called Helicobacter pylori and demonstrated that it could produce stomach ulcers, serious wounds in the stomach.
b. The researchers "produced one of the most radical and important changes in the last 50 years in the perception of a medical condition," said Lord Robert May, president of the Royal Society.

2.
a. He wanted to show that the bacterium caused stomach illness.
b. He got very sick.

3.
a. Ulcers could be cured quickly with a short course of antibiotics.
b. "I was treating my patients with the then-traditional methods for ulcers when his work was first published. I truly did not believe it until I saw what it did for my patients," said Dr. David Peura of the University of Virginia.

44 SB p. 136 Detecting Sequence with Sequence Markers

6.
a. 3
b. 1
c. 4
d. 2
e. 6
f. 5

Text 1 Secret Salary

7 SB p. 140 Active Previewing

A.
1. Graham Spanier
2. He has been able to keep his salary secret.
3. Pennsylvania State University

9 SB p. 142 Understanding the Text

A.
1. c
2. b
3. c

B.
1. $492,000
2. university-owned house and car
3. he ranks 25th among presidents of 139 public universities surveyed

11 SB p. 143 Understanding Apposition

1. He is president of Pennsylvania State University.
2. president of the Pennsylvania State University system
3. Graham Spanier is different from other public college presidents.
   He is president of the Pennsylvania State University system.
   Spanier has been able to keep his salary a secret for a long time.
4. Apposition enables the author to give the information in less space and without repeating the same information.

12 SB p. 143 Understanding the Main Idea

¶1: states the main idea
¶2: states the main idea
¶3: states the main idea
¶4: states the main idea
¶5: states the main idea

13 SB p. 144 Detecting Sequence with Sequence Markers

1. 1995, 1999, 2005
2. 1995, when Spanier was first hired; 1999, for tax reasons; 2005, because *The Chronicle of Higher Education* asked and because Spanier thought it was important
3. in 1995; in 1999; when it was . . .

14 SB p. 144 Understanding Subject Pronouns

A.
1. 9 times
2. 1: he
3. 3 times
4. 1: he

Text 2 Keeping Illness Secret

19 SB p. 145 Active Previewing

keeping an illness secret; should someone keep an illness secret

21 SB p. 147 Understanding the Text

A.
1. a
2. c
3. b

B.
1. yes
2. no
3. no
4. no
5. yes

23 SB p. 147 Scanning

1. chemotherapy
2. Elaine Benson
3. the Hamptons

24 SB p. 148 Understanding Vocabulary in Context—Definitions

A.

⬭ non-Hodgkin's lymphoma

definition: <u>a cancer of the lymphatic system</u>

25 SB p. 148 Understanding Possessive Adjectives and Object Pronouns

A.

1. Elaine Benson; 9 times
2. patients; once
3. Elaine Benson; once / Elaine Benson's daughter; once

B.

1. Everyone knew her and most people liked her. (¶1)
2. A visit to the doctor left her with a frightening diagnosis. (¶2)
3. They believed her. (¶2)
4. Elaine gave Kimberly two reasons why she wanted to hide her disease: she thought it would undermine the business, and she didn't want people feeling sorry for her. (¶3)
5. She says that her mother's hiding her illness was the only way she felt she could continue being herself. (¶6)

27 SB p. 149 Understanding Supporting Details

1. She would have been treated differently if people knew about her illness.
2. Patients say that the reason they don't tell about their illness is because they don't want pity but it's usually because they feel ashamed.
3. A lot of people were hurt because her mother didn't tell them about her disease.

Text 3 Secret Spenders

32 SB p. 150 Active Previewing

1. Secret Spenders; information about people's secrets as they relate to spending
2. Hiding Purchases; information about what people buy and hide / Hiding Amounts; information about how much they spend and hide / Hiding Financial Information; financial information that is hidden

34 SB p. 151 Scanning

1. b
2. a
3. c
4. b

Text 4 Lie Detection

39 SB p. 152 Active Previewing

1. lying and detecting lies
2. psychology class or a criminal justice class

41 SB p. 154 Understanding the Text

A.

1. c
2. b
3. b

B.

1, 2, 4, 5, 7

43 SB p. 155 Understanding Vocabulary in Context—Synonyms

¶2 lying / lie (noun): deception
¶4 liar (noun): fibber
¶4 lying / lie (verb): shade the truth
¶3 lying / lie (noun): fib
¶5 lying / lie (noun): deceitfulness

44 SB p. 156 Understanding Topic, Main Idea, and Supporting Details

A.

1. lying and lie detection
2. Studies have shown that it is nearly impossible for people to know whether someone is lying or not.

B.

1. People around the world share a stereotype for liars but it isn't true.
2. 2,000 people in 60 countries were asked a question./The most prevalent answer was that liars look away./Studies have shown that this isn't true./Liars don't shift around or look away.
3. There are some behaviors that liars tend to exhibit.
4. Fibbers move less./Their voices tend to be high./They make fewer errors./Their stories are "too good to be true."

45 SB p. 156 Understanding Vocabulary in Context—Examples

1. emotional clues
2. a smile, a grimace, a wince
3. such as

Notes

Notes

Notes

Notes

Notes